MW01643792

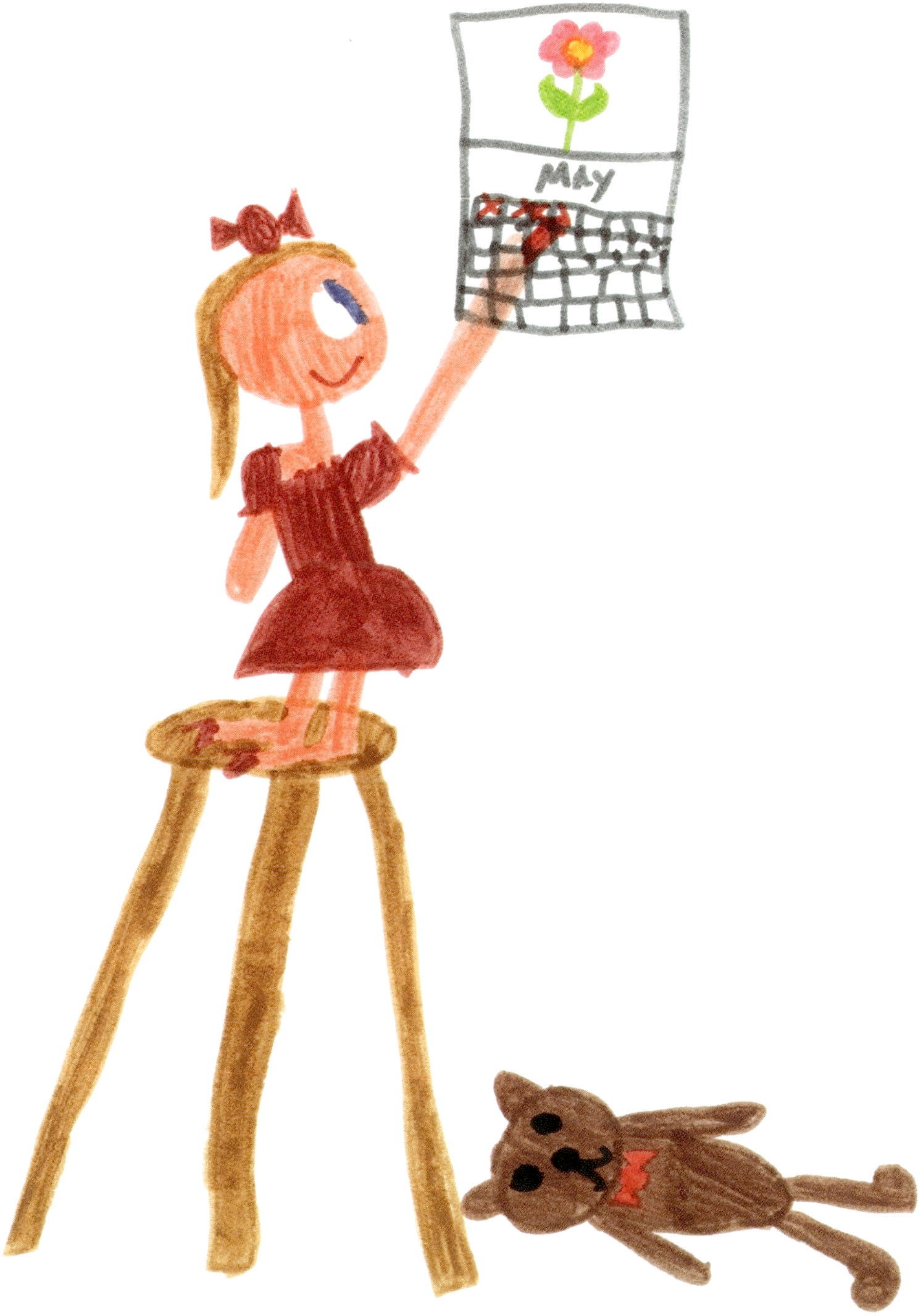

A Very Long Time

written by

Geri Timperley and Nikki Arro

illustrated by

Marlaina Kopietz

Interface Publishing
Minneapolis, Minnesota

ISBN-13: 978-0-9709443-9-9
ISBN-10: 0-9709443-9-X

Library of Congress Catalog Number: 2005929437

Printed in the United States of America

Second Printing: January 2006

10 09 08 07 06 JR 7 6 5 4 3 2

Cover and interior design by Rachel Holscher
Typesetting by Stanton Publication Services, Inc.

Interface Publishing
241 First Ave. N.
Minneapolis, MN 55401
(612) 338-8973
www.interfacepublishing.com

To order, visit www.averylongtime.com or call 1-866-630-9505. Reseller discounts available.

To all the men and women who are so bravely serving our country and to the families that support them and wait A VERY LONG TIME for their safe return.

One day at daycare a boy said to me,

"You don't have a dad!"

"Yes, I do," I said.

"Well, he never picks you up," he said.

I looked at him and said in my most grown-up voice,

"My daddy's at drill for . . ."

“. . . a very long time.”

I know about a very long time.

My mommy talks to me about it a lot.

Like when my mommy was waiting for

my daddy to ask her to marry him.

Mommy had to wait . . .

. . . a very long time.

Then, when my mommy found out that

she was going to have a baby,

she and my daddy had to wait for me to be born,

and they said it felt like . . .

. . . a very long time.

And when I ask my mommy,
"When is it going to be Christmas
or my birthday again?",
she always says, "In a little while."
'A little while' always takes . . .

. . . a very long time.

One day my daddy put me in his lap and
told me that he was going to help some people
and protect our country very far away.
My daddy said he was going to be gone for . . .

. . . a very long time.

On the morning my daddy left for his very long drill, my mommy and I got up very early. We took Daddy to a very big bus with all kinds of other daddies and mommies and kids too. When it was time to say goodbye, I hugged my daddy and said, “I will miss you for . . .”

“. . . a very long time.”

When my daddy was gone I got very lonely.

Grandma helped me make a paper chain with the number of weeks until my daddy would be home. We made . . .

. . . a very long chain.

Auntie Nikki had her students write letters
and draw pictures and bring treats for my daddy.
I helped her pack it all up. It went in a very big box.
Now my daddy would have enough
letters and treats to last . . .

. . . a very long time.

Sometimes I got very sad and wished my daddy was home. My mommy told me my daddy was helping make the world a safer and better place. She said lots of people in America and even the President would be very proud of my daddy for . . .

. . . a very long time.
The President's Garden

Mommy said that we needed to be brave like Daddy.

I made my daddy a picture and I told Mommy to write on it, “I am brave like you, Daddy!”

I kept asking, “Daddy, did you get my picture yet?”

He said the mail takes . . .

. . . a very long time.

I waited and waited and counted the days
on a calendar until my daddy would come home.
It would be two birthdays and one Christmas.
That means I had to wait . . .

. . . a very long time.

Finally, Mommy said that we were going to
the airport to pick up Daddy. I asked the whole way,
"Are we there yet, Mommy?" She said,
"Not yet!", even though we had been
riding in the car for . . .

. . . a very long time.
USA
AIRPORT
OFFICE

When all the people were getting off the plane I watched and waited for my daddy. I saw him walking way down the ramp. I ran as fast as I could and jumped into his arms. My daddy hugged me and kissed me and cried with me for . . .

. . . a very long time.

The next day Daddy brought me to daycare.

I tell everyone that my daddy has come home.

I am so happy that my daddy is home.

Now he will be mine FOREVER, and that is . . .

. . . A VERY LONG TIME!

The End.